Published in the UK in 1994 by
Schofield & Sims Limited, Huddersfield, England.

0 7217 5008 7

FIRST IMPRESSIONS

Sea Creatures

Schofield & Sims Limited Huddersfield.

Some Sea Creatures

Ray

Pipe-fish

Sea slug

Parrot fish

Sea urchin

Spider crab

Leopard shark

Brill

Moray eel

Manatee

White whale

Cuttlefish

Nautilus

Jellyfish

Starfish

Turtle

Toadfish

Swordfish

Sponge

3

The Whale

The blue whale is the largest marine *mammal* in the world. It usually lives in cold polar waters. At the end of the summer, whales travel to warmer waters where the females give birth, usually to a single calf.

Some whales have no teeth. Instead, their mouths contain thin strips of whalebone which filter the sea water to catch *plankton* and tiny shrimps called krill.

Other whales, such as the sperm whale and the white whale, have formidable teeth. They eat fish and squid.

A baby whale weighs 1000 kilograms at birth and drinks 500 litres of milk a day! The female will risk her life to protect her baby from sharks or hunters.

The whale has an opening called a blow-hole on its head. When it needs to breathe, a whale comes to the surface and breathes in air through its blow-hole. The blow-hole closes when the whale dives.

The Dolphin

The dolphin is also a *mammal*. A highly intelligent animal, it is known as the sailor's friend and has often been said to have saved people from drowning. Dolphins have their own language, which perhaps humans will understand one day.

The dolphin has a keen sense of hearing. This helps it to *locate* distant objects and also to find its way at night.

Dolphins have very sensitive skin. They love to be touched and like to rub against one another.

Dolphins travel in a group called a school. The female dolphins and babies are in the middle of the school, protected by the males and the younger dolphins.

The killer whale is a large dolphin that feeds on large fish and on smaller dolphins, seals and walruses.

The Seal

The seal is a *mammal* which lives mainly in the icy waters around the North Pole. Its body is perfectly adapted to life at sea because its four paws have turned into flippers. It lives on fish, *molluscs* and shellfish.

The baby seal has a thick white coat that protects it from the cold. This is why it is known as a 'whitecoat'.

Before diving, the seal empties its lungs of air. Seals can stay under the water for five minutes without breathing.

The huge walrus is a cousin of the seal. It has two curved teeth called tusks, which can be 60 centimetres long.

The elephant seal weighs over 3000 kilograms and is 6 metres long – the length of a large car!

The Shark

People have always been fascinated and frightened by sharks. However, most of these large fish are not dangerous. Some sharks do attack occasionally, usually when they feel threatened or when their territory is invaded.

The shark has powerful jaws and several rows of razor-sharp teeth.

The shark's hearing and sense of smell are very highly developed. Its keen eyesight allows it to see at night.

The hammerhead shark gets its name from the shape of its head. Its eyes and nostrils are situated at the ends of the 'hammer'.

The whale shark is the largest fish in the world. This shark has 310 rows of teeth, but it is not dangerous to humans.

The Ray

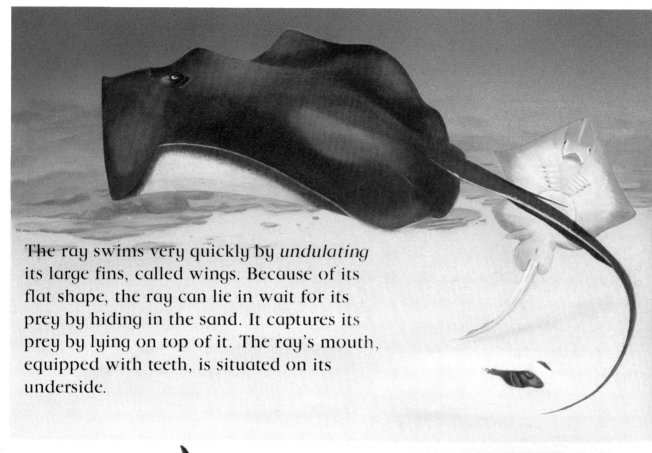

The ray swims very quickly by *undulating* its large fins, called wings. Because of its flat shape, the ray can lie in wait for its prey by hiding in the sand. It captures its prey by lying on top of it. The ray's mouth, equipped with teeth, is situated on its underside.

The manta ray is a type of 'flying' fish that lives near the surface of the sea and leaps out of the water. It can weigh almost 2000 kilograms.

The electric ray, or torpedo fish, paralyses its victim with an electric shock. This fish needs to recharge itself, like a battery, before it can attack again.

The Octopus

Shy and cautious, the octopus lives in small underwater caves. When it leaves its cave to hunt, it hides among the rocks and corals. The octopus has a kind of horny beak which is strong enough to break open a crab's shell.

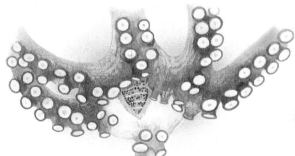

The octopus crawls along by using its eight tentacles which are covered in suckers.

When surprised by an enemy, the octopus immediately releases a cloud of black ink to give itself time to escape.

The Turtle

The leathery turtle is the largest marine turtle. It can swim very quickly because its front legs form huge fins. The turtle has powerful jaws and feeds on fish, jellyfish and other soft-bodied creatures.

Although it spends its life in the water, the leathery turtle lays its eggs on land. The female buries them in the sand, and then returns to the sea.

The baby turtles hatch after seven or eight weeks. They rush towards the sea as fast as they can to escape from the birds waiting to eat them.

14

The Sea Horse

The sea horse lives among water plants. It attaches itself to these by its tail. Its body is covered with a bony armour. When it eats, the sea horse acts like a vacuum cleaner and sucks up small sea creatures and tiny fish.

The sea horse is the only fish that swims in an upright position. It has a fan-shaped fin on its back which propels it through the water.

The male sea horse has a pouch on his stomach, just like the kangaroo. The female lays her eggs in the pouch and the young ones live in it until they are mature.

The Salmon

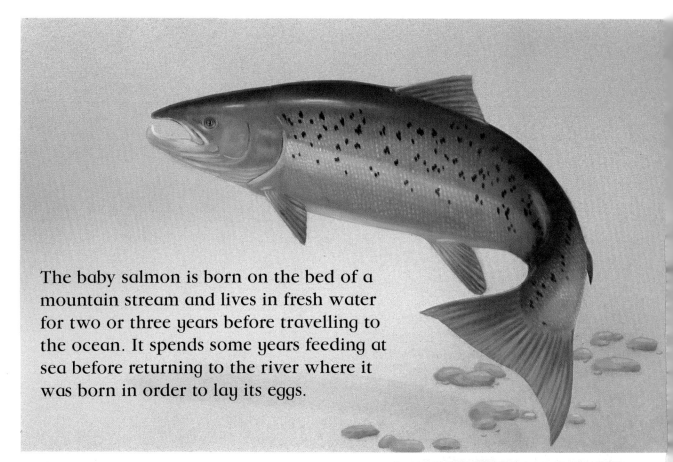

The baby salmon is born on the bed of a mountain stream and lives in fresh water for two or three years before travelling to the ocean. It spends some years feeding at sea before returning to the river where it was born in order to lay its eggs.

The eggs hatch after about 50 days. Many of the young salmon are eaten by fish or birds.

Dams across rivers sometimes prevent the salmon from swimming upstream. To help the fish, a kind of staircase, called a fish ladder, is built for the salmon to use.

The Eel

Although it looks like a snake, the eel is a fish. A great traveller, it spends part of its life in the fresh water of rivers and marshes before travelling across the Atlantic Ocean to lay its eggs.

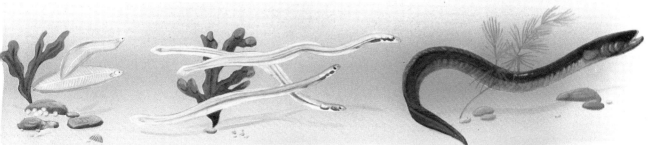

The egg produces a larva which travels back across the Atlantic. When it gets near the coast, the larva turns into a transparent elver, or young eel, which swims into the rivers and marshes.

It now takes the true shape of an eel. When it is fully grown, the eel changes itself again to adapt to the ocean depths. Its skin thickens and its eyes grow larger.

Crustaceans

Crustaceans are sea creatures which have a hard shell. They inhabit the rocky areas in or near the sea. The body of a crustacean is covered with a jointed *carapace*. They have feelers which are sensitive to movement, taste and smell. Some crustaceans have claws.

The crab walks sideways. Its powerful claws are formidable weapons.

The shrimp can change colour so that it blends in with its surroundings and cannot be easily seen.

The hermit-crab has a very thin shell, so it usually lives inside an empty whelk shell. Often, a sea anemone will grow on the shell.

To grow bigger, a lobster has to shed its shell. The lobster comes out of its shell backwards, then it eats the old shell as it waits for the new one to harden.

Corals

The brightly-coloured corals look like plants. In fact, they are tiny creatures which live in *colonies*. Most of them live in warm waters, where they build rocky barriers, called reefs.

To grow, corals need sunlight as well as clear water that remains at the same temperature.

Some corals eat worms, larvae and eggs. They catch them with their *poisonous* tentacles, which paralyse their prey.

The sea anemone looks like a flower, but it comes from the same family as the coral. Sea anemones live on rocks or in the sand on the seabed.

The mouth of a sea anemone is situated in the middle of its tentacles, like the heart of a flower. Sea anemones feed on fish and shrimps.

Shellfish

Shellfish live in every ocean and reproduce by laying eggs. Some shellfish have a single shell, often spiral shaped, such as the winkle or the nautilus. Others have a shell formed by two halves, such as the oyster or the mussel.

The shell protects the soft body of the *mollusc* inside.

The tiger cowrie fights off its enemies by shooting out a jet of acid that burns their eyes.

The scallop can swim backwards as well as forwards. This helps it to escape from its main enemies – the starfish and the octopus.

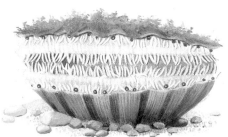

The scallop has lots of little blue eyes which detect movement. When one eye is destroyed, it is replaced by another one.

Some Strange Fish

Narwhal
The narwhal is a whale which lives in the cold waters of the Arctic. The male has a spiral tusk three metres long on its forehead.

Sunfish
From the side, this fish is round, like the sun. It often lies on its side and lets itself float to the surface of the ocean.

Gulper Eel
The gulper eel gets its name from its enormous mouth, which is shaped like a funnel. The eel's mouth cavity is larger than its body! It has a long, tapering tail.

Lantern Fish
These fish have small luminous organs on their heads and bodies, to help them to see in the dark waters where they live.

Flying Fish
To escape from their enemies, flying fish can leap out of the water and spread out their large fins to glide over the waves.

Sawfish
The muzzle of this fish is shaped like a saw. It uses this to scrape about in the sand for food.

Stonefish
The stonefish is the most *poisonous* fish of all. One prick of its spines can be fatal.

Puffer-fish
This spiny fish inflates itself with air to become a prickly ball of spines. It is also called the porcupine fish.

Glossary

Carapace
The hard upper shell of some creatures, such as the crab or the tortoise.

Colony
A collection of plants or animals living close together.

Locate
To find out the position of something.

Mammal
An animal which feeds its young with its own milk. The whale, the dolphin and the seal are mammals – so are humans.

Mollusc
A type of shellfish with a soft body and often a hard shell. A snail is a mollusc.

Plankton
The tiny animals and plants that live near the surface of the sea.

Poisonous
Containing a substance that can make you very ill, or even kill.

Undulate
To move up and down with a waving motion.